MUSIC FOR SAXOPHONE

by Jorge Polanuer

ISBN 978-1-57424-248-5
SAN 683-8022

Cover by James Creative Group

Cover saxophone image courtesy of
Greatmind Saxaphones   www.greatmind-sax.com

Copyright © 2009 CENTERSTREAM Publishing, LLC
P.O. Box 17878 - Anaheim Hills, CA 92817

www.centerstream-usa.com

Acknowledgements

The following people participated in the recording:

Sax, flute, arrangements and composition: Jorge Polanuer

Piano: Juanjo Hermida, Ramiro Allende

Guitar: Egardo Cardozo, Guillermo Capocci

Drums: Marcelo Mira, Gustavo López, Ricardo Arenhaldt

Percussion: Hubert Reyes, Giovani Berti, Fernando Jazan , Paulo Nascimento

Bajo: Ricardo Baumgarten

Cavaquinho: Deryck Santos

The author wished to acknowledge the valuable contributions of:

CUATRO VIENTOS, Monica Cabouli, Alejandra Bausano, Delia Adeff, Jaime Polanuer, Fernando Jazán, Santiago Vegas, Diego Heras ,Cecilia Zoppi, Omar Riemersma, Daniel Piekar y Guillermo Capocci.

Table of Contents & ⊙ Track List

About the Author

Jorge Polanuer (11/29/60)

Saxophone player, flutist, composer, arranger, and teacher. Received his degree as Flute Professor in 1983 at the National conservatory of Music

"Carlos Lopez Buchardo", the most prestigious institution in Argentina. He has been a member of the musical-theater group **Cuatro Vientos** <u>www. cuatrovientos.com.ar</u> since 1987. With this group, he participated in numerous international festivals, including Madrid, Lisbon, Miami, Mexico, Venezuela, Costa Rica, Bolivia and Brasil, and recorded five CDs in which other renowned performers have participated: Les Luthiers, Andrés Calamaro, Chango Spasiuk, and Bob Telson.

Prior to co-founding **Cuatro Vientos**, he took part in various Jazz, Fusion, Classical Music, and Rock groups, among them "Los Abuelos de la Nada" , and Andrés Calamaro´s band, with whom he recorded four CDs. Jorge has also composed the music for several theater plays: "Gala" *, "Shakespeare´s Merry Women", "Shakespiriando", "Sinvergüenzas" (No shame), "Cuatro Vientos y el Saxo Mágico"* (Cuatro Vientos and the magic sax), "Alma de Saxofón" * (Saxophone soul), "La Tempestad" * (The storm) , and "Sudestada" *Available on CD. He won the "Premio ACE (Asoc. Cronistas del Espectáculo) 2000" (the most important music award in Argentina) on best original music for theater.

In 2001, he was invited by SAXOPHONE JOURNAL (the most prestigious magazine for saxophone players) to do a ROCK MASTER CLASS.

He is an endorser for VANDOREN reeds.

*The air belongs to us all
air lets us play sax
the sax lets us make music
music lets us touch the air.
And this MUSIC FOR SAX,
which I felt mine when I composed it
Will be yours when you play it,
And will be everybody's when the air sounds
Play it, enjoy it, listen to it,*

and tell me about it later.

jorge@cuatrovientos.com.ar   www.cuatrovientos.com.ar   www.autores.org.ar/jpolanuer

Introduction

This book is made up of tunes developed specifically with the sax in mind, inspired in the main rhythms of the Americas; these enable us to experience a broad range of sensations.

COCONUT TUNES and *THE ISLAND:* a retrospective look at the Old Havannah, with all the flavor of Cuban Salsa, a walk through the history of one of America's most enigmatic cultures.

MY BABY CALL : a sweet, bluesy ballad, a summons to deploy all the sensuality of the sax .

BLUES BUG: the broad sensaation of a classic blues with the necessary space for you to let your imagination go and improvise.

A NEIGHBOR AND SAMBA FOR NOT SLEEPING: all the charm of the SAMBA, the typical music of (Brasil).

HOOP HOOP: a kind of bolero composed for a circus show called GALA, that was used for a scene in which the hoop was the main element.

MY KINGDOM FOR A SAX: Inspired by Dixieland, reminiscent of the musical climate of those days.

LITTLE CORNER: A milonga, one of the many variations of the Buenos Aires tango, characteristic of the early 20th century.

THE ENCOUNTER: a pleasant ballad in duet form, in which the alto and the tenor saxes tease and seduce each other. Besides the audio, the CD has a track to play the tune as a duet, another just for the tenor, and another for the contraalto.

MARTIN'S CANDOMBE: a popular Afro-Uruguayan rhythm. I originally composed this tune for my son Martín when he was 2 months old.

A crucial point when playing any instrument is to respect the articulations, which is a fundamental variable for wind instruments: the equivalent in spoken language would be the relationship between vowels and consonants, i.e. diction. This is how we get the instrument to "sing", and our ideas can flow freely and faithfully.

I suggest the following order for approaching each tune:

1. Read the tune with all the details (notes, rhythm, articulations, effects) without the accompaniment.

2. Listen to the audio of the tune, and try to imitate my way of playing and my attitude.

3. Play the tune with the accompaniment.

1. COCONUT TUNES
Salsa

audio: 1 / play alone: 14

Jorge Polanuer

1. COCONUT TUNES
Salsa

audio: 1 / play alone: 14

Jorge Polanuer

9

2. MY BABY CALL
Blues ballad

SWING

Jorge Polanuer

audio: 2 / play alone: 15

improv.

2. MY BABY CALL
Blues ballad

SWING

Jorge Polanuer

audio: 2 / play alone: 15

improv.

Am   Am/G

F   E^7 Am Am/G   F   E^7 Am Am/G

3. BLUES BUG
Blues

SWING

audio: 3 / play alone: 16

Jorge Polanuer

3. BLUES BUG
Blues

SWING

Jorge Polanuer

audio: 3 / play alone: 16

4. A NEIGHBOR
samba (brasil)

audio: 4 / play alone: 17

Jorge Polanuer

4. A NEIGHBOR
samba (brasil)

audio: 4 / play alone: 17

Jorge Polanuer

5.THE ISLAND
Salsa

audio:5 / play alone: 18

Jorge Polanuer

5. THE ISLAND
Salsa

audio:5 / play alone: 18

Jorge Polanuer

6. HOOP HOOP
Bolero

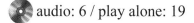audio: 6 / play alone: 19

Jorge Polanuer

6. HOOP HOOP
Bolero

audio: 6 / play alone: 19

Jorge Polanuer

7. MY KINGDOM FOR A SAX
Jazz

SWING

audio: 7 / play alone: 20

Jorge Polanuer

alto

ritardando

7. MY KINGDOM FOR A SAX
Jazz

SWING

audio: 7 / play alone: 21

Jorge Polanuer

ritardando

8. LITTLE CORNER

Milonga

Jorge Polanuer

audio: 8 / play alone: 21

8. LITTLE CORNER
Milonga

audio: 8 / play alone: 21

Jorge Polanuer

9. SAMBA FOR NOT SLEEPING
samba (brasil)

audio: 9 / play alone: 22

Jorge Polanuer

9. SAMBA FOR NOT SLEEPING
samba (brasil)

Jorge Polanuer

10. BALLOONS
Reggae

audio: 10 / play alone: 23

Jorge Polanuer

alto

10. BALLOONS
Reggae

audio: 10 / play alone: 23

Jorge Polanuer

tenor

11. THE ENCOUNTER
Duet ballad for alto and tenor saxophone

swing

audio: 11 / play alone to duet: 24 / to tenor: 25 / to alto: 26

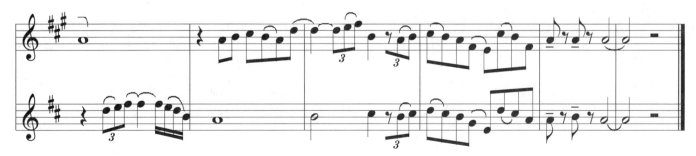

12. MARTIN'S CANDOMBE
Candombe

audio: 12 / play alone: 27

Jorge Polanuer

alto

12. MARTIN'S CANDOMBE
Candombe

audio: 12 / play alone: 27

Jorge Polanuer

More Great Saxophone Books from Jorge Polanuer...

SAXOPHONE STYLES
by Jorge Polanuer

This cool book/CD pack lets saxophonists play along in a variety of styles, such as rock, salsa, reggae, chorinho, chamané, funk, soul, and gospel.

00000242 Book/CD Pack $17.95

TANGO SOLOS FOR SAXOPHONE
by Jorge Polanuer

composer and teacher Jorge Polanuer says in the intro to this book, "Tango is not for the spineless." So, if you're feeling brave and ready to unleash the emotion of this passionate music, get your sax and play along with the 12 great tunes in this book! The CD features full recordings of Jorge and his saxophone quartet "Cuatro Vientos," plus accompaniment-only tracks. For tenor and alto players.

00000275 Book/CD Pack $19.95

P.O. Box 17878 - Anaheim Hills, CA 92817

(714) 779-9390   www.centerstream-usa.com

More Great Saxophone from Centerstream...

The Competition

Those using
Centerstream
Books & DVDs